Rachel Carson was a scientist and an author.

Cornerstones of Freedom

The Story of
RACHEL CARSON
AND THE ENVIRONMENTAL MOVEMENT

By Leila Merrell Foster, JD., PhD.

CHILDRENS PRESS®
CHICAGO

Crop duster airplanes spray pesticides over wide areas.

Library of Congress Cataloging-in-Publication Data

Foster, Leila Merrell.

  The story of Rachel Carson and the environmental
movement / by Leila M. Foster.
    p.   cm. — (Cornerstones of freedom)
  Summary: Describes the life of ecologist Rachel Carson,
with emphasis on the importance of her books for the
environmental movement.
  ISBN 0-516-04753-1
  1. Carson, Rachel, 1907-1964—Juvenile literature.
2. Ecologists—United States—Biography—Juvenile
literature. 3. Women conservationists—United
States—Biography—Juvenile literature. [1. Carson,
Rachel, 1907-1964. 2. Conservationists. 3. Biologists.]
I. Title. II. Series.
QH31.C33F67 1990
333.7′2′092—dc20
[B]   90-2208
[92]   CIP
                                           AC

PHOTO CREDITS

Cover—Portrait bust by Una
    Hanbury in the National Portrait
    Gallery, photograph taken by
    Shirley A. Briggs, © Rachel
    Carson Council, Inc. (foreground)

AP/Wide World Photos—3, 17
    (right), 23 (right), 26, 27

Beinecke Library/Yale
    University—7 (left), 9 (left), 10
    (left), 14 (left)

The Bettmann Archive—1

Used by permission of the Rachel
    Carson Council, Inc.: 7 (right), 8,
    23 (left), 28 (inset), 30
    © Erich Hartmann—2, 28
    (background)
    Shirley A. Briggs—14 (right), 17
    (left), 25, 32

Chatham College—9 (right), 10
    (right)

Magnum Photos:
    © Erich Hartmann—20

National Marine Fisheries Center
    Archive—11

Photri—21

Root Resources: 24
    © Jack Monsarratt—4

Shostal/SuperStock International—
    13

Tom Stack and Associates:
    © Gary Milburn—6
    © John Cancalosi—31 (inset)
    © Brian Parker—31
    (background)

TSW, Click/Chicago Ltd.:
    © Ulli Seer—cover (background)
    © Glenn Knudsen—18 (left)

U.S. Fish and Wildlife Service—18
    (right)

Page 3: Some plant pests can be controlled by sprays
containing genetically altered bacteria, which attack
the pests.

At a press conference on August 29, 1962, a reporter asked President John F. Kennedy this question: "Mr. President, there appears to be a growing concern among scientists as to the possibility of dangerous long-range effects from the use of DDT and other pesticides. Have you considered asking the Department of Agriculture or the Public Health Service to take a closer look at this?"

President Kennedy replied, "Yes, and I know that they already are. I think particularly, of course, since Miss Carson's book, but they are examining the matter."

Can one person really make a difference in the world around us? Yes. Rachel Carson was such a person. As a scientist, she was one of the first to warn us that substances we use endanger our environment. As a writer, she was able to paint vivid word pictures that help us appreciate the beauty of the world in which we live.

Words like *environmental concerns* and *ecology* (the relationship of living things to their environment) were not widely used when Rachel Carson began to write. The dangers of pesticides (poisons used to kill pests) were not generally known. Her book *Silent Spring* helped make us aware of our

Pollution from a pulp and paper mill clogs a waterway.

need to act responsibly to avoid harming the world in which we live. If we do not take care, we could lose all the birds and insects and have a silent spring. A twenty-fifth anniversary edition of *Silent Spring* was issued in 1987, with a new foreword by Paul Brooks, the editor of the first edition.

> By awakening us to a specific danger—the poisoning of the earth with chemicals—she has helped us to recognize many other ways (some little known in her time) in which mankind is degrading the quality of life on our planet. And *Silent Spring* will continue to remind us that in our overorganized and overmechanized age, individual initiative and courage still count: change can be brought about, not through incitement to war or violent revolution, but rather by altering the direction of thinking about the world we live in.

6

It took courage to write *Silent Spring*. Rachel Carson had to struggle to make a mass of scientific facts meaningful. She was attacked by those who disagreed with her and by those who stood to gain from continued use of pesticides.

Rachel Carson was born on May 27, 1907, in Springdale, Pennsylvania. She grew up on some 65 acres of land on the outskirts of Springdale, among apple trees, woods, and fields. Although they were not a farming family, the Carsons kept cows, horses and chickens. Besides her mother and father, her family consisted of a sister, Marian, who was ten years older than Rachel, and a brother, Robert, eight years older.

Left: Mrs. Carson with her children Marian, Rachel, and Robert.
Right: Young Rachel with flowers

Rachel with her dog Candy

Rachel was a shy girl. She was closest to her mother, from whom she inherited an interest in the world of nature. Often the little girl would spend time alone in the woods, learning about the flowers, insects, and birds. She missed many days at school because of illness, but her mother tutored her, so Rachel kept up with her studies.

A great reader, Rachel wanted to become a writer. When she was 10 years old, she had a story accepted for publication in *St. Nicholas*, a popular magazine for children. Her work won a prize called the Silver Badge, which Rachel Carson said brought her more joy than all the checks she later received for her best-selling books. Her other stories and essays were purchased for publication by *St. Nicholas* magazine—at the rate of a penny a word. Rachel also wrote poetry, but her poems were never published.

Although Rachel had few close childhood friends, she was not disliked by her classmates. In her high-school yearbook, this description appears next to Rachel's photograph:

> Rachel's like the mid-day sun
> Always very bright
> Never stops her studying
> 'Till she gets it right.

Left: Rachel with her mother and father.
Right: Rachel (top row, second from right) and her teammates played on the college Honorary Hockey Team.

With an annual scholarship of $100 toward her tuition, Rachel went to the Pennsylvania College for Women (now Chatham College). She became an English major and joined the literary club and the staff of the student paper. At the end of her sophomore year, she was required to take a course in biology (the study of plants and animals). The subject fascinated her so much that she wondered if she should became a scientist instead of a writer. In the middle of her junior year, Rachel switched her major to zoology (the study of animals). In her senior year, she was elected president of the science club.

Left: Rachel (right) and her college biology professor, Mary Skinker.
Right: Rachel Carson's senior portrait

Rachel showed concern for others. Once her classmates criticized a biology teacher who never spoke
to anyone in the halls. Rachel explained that the
teacher was very nearsighted and it was necessary
for other people to speak first to be recognized.

Graduating with highest honors from college in
1928, Rachel earned a master's degree at Johns
Hopkins University and later taught zoology at
Johns Hopkins and the University of Maryland. Her
summer studies at Woods Hole Marine Biological
Laboratory in Massachusetts increased her interest
in the sea.

10

When critics later claimed that Rachel was not a trained biologist, Paul Brooks, the editor of *Silent Spring*, said, "For them [the critics] should be reserved a special corner in the Library of Hell, equipped with a barnacle-covered bench and a whale-oil lamp, by whose light they would be compelled to read out loud from her master's thesis: 'The Development of the Pronephros During the Embryonic and Early Larval Life of the Catfish (*Ictalurus punctatus*).' "

Rachel began writing articles on fisheries for the *Baltimore Sunday Sun*, and she continued her part-time teaching. When her father died in 1935, leaving little money to support her mother and herself, Rachel looked for other employment. Although jobs were hard to find during those depression years, she was in luck. The Bureau of Fisheries was looking for someone who could write short radio scripts, which the staff called Seven-Minute Fish Tales, although the more glamorous official name was "Romance Under the Waters." The chief of the biology division, Elmer Higgins, charged with this project was desperately looking for someone with both scientific and writing skills. When Rachel Carson asked about the job, she was hired on a part-time basis.

The next year her older sister died at the age of

Elmer Higgins, chief of the biology division of the Bureau of Fisheries

40, leaving two school-age children, Marjorie and Virginia, who were taken into the Carson household. Fortunately, the opportunity for a full-time position as a "junior aquatic biologist" at the Bureau of Fisheries opened up. Rachel Carson took the civil service examination. She was the only woman competing for the job, and she had the highest score. She was hired at a salary of $2,000 a year and was given an office on an inside courtyard from which she could barely see the sky.

After the radio series ended, Rachel was asked to write something general about the sea. When she finished, she showed it to her chief. He told her that he didn't think it was suitable for the Bureau of Fisheries, but he encouraged her to send it to the *Atlantic Monthly* magazine.

Rachel Carson followed this advice. The piece was published in the September 1937 issue with the title "Undersea." The beauty that characterizes her later writing shows through in this early article:

> Who has known the ocean? Neither you nor I, with our earth-bound senses, know the foam and surge of the tide that beats over the crab hiding under the seaweed of his tide-pool home; or the lilt of the long, slow swells of mid-ocean, where shoals of wandering fish prey and are preyed upon, and the dolphin breaks the waves to breathe the upper atmosphere.

The rocky
coast of
Maine

The fascination that would lead her to write about the sea and the shoreline also is foreshadowed:

> The ocean is a place of paradoxes. It is the home of the great white shark, two-thousand-pound killer of the seas, and of the hundred-foot blue whale, the largest animal that ever lived. It is also the home of living things so small that your two hands might scoop up as many of them as there are stars in the Milky Way.

Two people who read "Undersea" encouraged Rachel Carson to write books. Quincy Howe, an editor and publisher, wrote to enquire whether she would be interested in discussing a book project. Hendrik Willem van Loon, a famous author, invited her to his home and arranged a meeting with Mr. Howe. After a dinner with the Van Loon family and a visit to the publisher's office the next day, Rachel began work on the book *Under the Sea Wind*.

This first book was one of her favorites. Many of

Left: A draft manuscript page from *Under the Sea Wind*.
Right: Rachel Carson examines a tidal pool near her home in Maine.

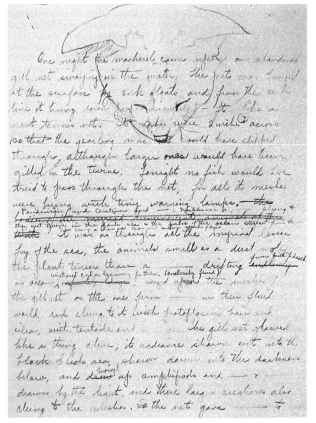

her friends agreed. She presented scientific facts by telling stories. To meet her deadline, Rachel often wrote late at night. Her two Persian cats, Buzzie and Kito, kept her company. The manuscript was completed by the end of 1940. The book was published on November 1, 1941—just weeks before the entry of the United States into World War II on December 7. Rachel Carson was disappointed with the sales of the book—less than 1,600 copies were sold in the first six years—but she was pleased with the reviews, especially the praise of scientists, who were often unhappy with scientific books written for a popular audience.

Rachel Carson was busy during the war years. She wrote pamphlets to help people plan wartime menus using fish with which they might not be familiar. Fish was an important source of protein when other foods were in short supply. She also was trying to write articles for popular magazines. Although the war years were busy ones, Rachel Carson looked back on her early years in Washington, D.C., as carefree.

When things got too dull at the office, Ms. Carson and her fellow workers enjoyed some practical jokes. On one occasion, they were going to telegraph one of the employees in the Chicago office of their agency and say that a famous feature writer and a photographer were arriving to do a story about the employee's cookbook. The writer was to insist that the main dish had to be field mice for twelve, served with mushrooms and wine. Their practical joke was never carried out because they could not legally send off the telegram in someone else's name.

After the war, when travel was possible again, Ms. Carson traveled to bird sanctuaries and to the Everglades in Florida. In the summer months she rented a cabin on a river near Boothbay, Maine. There she had a ten- to twelve-foot tidal area to study. Later, she used the money from her writing to buy a cottage near West Southport in Maine.

When her government work became a little easier, Rachel began work on a manuscript that was to be her best-selling *The Sea Around Us*. At the invitation of Dr. William Beebe, a distinguished undersea explorer, she put on a diving suit for a look at the ocean underwater. She also spent ten days on the *Albatross III*, observing scientific studies of the fish population in certain areas. Her real work, however, was collecting the scientific data and translating that material into language that would convey the beauty and wonder of the ocean. She chose a straight narrative approach this time. The final manuscript was delivered to her publisher in July 1950.

Left: Rachel on the research boat *Nauplius*, with a diving helmet for exploring underwater. Right: Rachel Carson (second from right) receiving the nonfiction National Book Award for *The Sea Around Us* in 1952

Money was still very tight for the Carson family. Her professional friends helped Rachel secure two fellowship awards of money for writers. Rachel hoped to sell chapters of the book to magazines, but many magazines rejected the manuscript before the *Yale Review* bought one chapter. The article won an award as the best example of science writing for the year. The book itself won the John Burroughs Medal for natural history writing from scientists and the National Book Award from publishers.

Left: A tidal pool on the southern Maine coast.
Right: Rachel Carson (above) studying sea life
at the shoreline

That a nonfiction book about the sea would become a best-seller surprised most publishers. When her first book, *Under the Sea Wind*, was reissued, it also made the best-seller list. Few authors ever had two nonfiction books on the best-seller list at the same time, but Rachel Carson did. Besides the money, honorary degrees and awards came her way. A movie based on *The Sea Around Us* was made. Although Rachel did not approve of the script because it contained scientific errors, the film was released. The movie later won an Oscar for the best full-length documentary film.

Like most writers, Rachel Carson was already working on her next book. *The Edge of the Sea* was to be a guide to the seashore life on the Atlantic coast. It turned out to be more than a guide that simply tells the difference between specimens. It is a personal essay that helps the reader understand the lives of the inhabitants of the coastline.

She had received a Guggenheim fellowship to begin the fieldwork for her new book, and she took a year's leave of absence from her job as Biologist and Chief Editor. In 1952, before the year was up, she resigned from the Bureau of Fisheries. The money from her books allowed her to devote all her time to her writing. By the end of 1953, she was protesting what she saw happening in the government—professionals were being replaced by political appointees in important government positions such as the director of the Fish and Wildlife Service.

While *The Edge of the Sea* was a best-seller, it is not as popular today as Rachel's other books—perhaps because of its more limited scope. Rachel wrote a TV script for a show about the sky, and

Rachel and her adopted son, Roger

became interested in microscopic photography. She also wrote an article for *Woman's Home Companion* entitled "Help Your Child to Wonder." The article emphasizes the wonder that the child and the adult can experience in nature. It does not require the knowledge of a scientist—simply the eyes of the observer looking for beauty. Rachel had used this approach to introduce her niece's son, Roger, to the wonders of the world around him. When her niece died, Rachel Carson adopted Roger and thus became mother to a five-year-old. Her own mother, then 88, also required her attention because of an arthritic condition. When her mother died in 1958, Rachel Carson lost the person who first encouraged her to write and inspired her to fight against what she thought wrong.

Many people warned Rachel not to attempt her next project. While the beauty and wonder of nature might well be suited to her poetic style, would readers buy a book on pesticides? Rachel had doubts of her own. However, her anguish about the misuse of nature by humans was fundamental to her attitude toward life. As a scientist—and now as a well-known author—she had access to the solid facts that would have to be incorporated into the book. She never claimed that the ideas in *Silent Spring* were only her own. She sought out experts in many fields to determine the damage to human health and to the lives of birds, insects, fish, and other animals by the indiscriminate use of pesticides. Her position was never that all use of pesticides should be banned.

Dead fish on the shore are a sign of water pollution.

She argued that the hazards of pesticide use must be sufficiently weighed before the application of such chemicals could be approved. Her skills as a biologist enabled her to comprehend and consolidate the technical data supplied to her by the experts.

Some hint of future problems and the attitude of the public toward the use of pesticides came when her local community had to decide whether or not to spray the trees against insects. Rachel Carson was to speak at a community meeting on the subject. Shortly before the meeting, one of her neighbors telephoned to tell Rachel that she was an alarmist and should not believe all she read about pesticides. Rachel responded by giving a speech that one observer noted could not be called "gentle." She won. The vote was against spraying.

Rachel was anxious to get her book into print because she felt that it would be news to 99 percent of the public, but a number of serious illnesses slowed her down. She had a tumor removed from her breast. Later, she learned that, although she had not been told when she asked, the tumor was malignant. Now there was evidence that the cancer had spread. After four years of work, the book was finished in 1962. Rachel Carson had written it to alert her generation to the hazards of pesticides, but she had

The Carson family pets (left) relax on the porch steps in 1920.
Rachel (right) with a copy of *Silent Spring*.

kept her eye on larger issues: "Future generations are unlikely to condone our lack of prudent concern for the integrity of the natural world that supports all life."

The book became a landmark in our environmental history. Rachel's thorough research withstood the attacks from the opposition. She wrote from her heart because the issues were central to her philosophy of life, which had been based on the "reverence for life" concept of Albert Schweitzer, the European theologian and medical missionary to Africa. *Silent Spring* is dedicated to Schweitzer.

A farmer sprays a bean field with pesticides.

Who would oppose her ideas? It must be remembered that most people, lacking the scientist's understanding of the complex data, did not recognize the dangers. Many thought that Ms. Carson was urging a return to the days when crop failures and plagues were widespread and there was no means of preventing them. Farmers feared their crop yields would be diminished, and they preferred to use pesticides and didn't mind if that meant there would be fewer birds around to eat their crops. Medical information about the long-term effects on human health could be disputed because of the relatively short time some of the chemicals had been in use. Opposition came from the chemical industry, agriculture groups, the Nutrition Foundation, and the American Medical Association.

The attacks were not always limited to the facts. In a 1962 speech to the Women's National Press Club, Rachel Carson reported on some of these tactics: "One obvious way to try to weaken a cause is to discredit the person who champions it. So—the masters of invective and insinuation have been busy: I am 'a bird lover—a cat lover—a fish lover,' a priestess of nature, a devotee of a mystical cult having to do with laws of the universe which my critics consider themselves immune to. Another well-known, and much-used, device is to misrepresent my position and attack the things I have never said."

Rachel Carson watching migrating hawks on Hawk Mountain, Pennsylvania, in 1946

Rachel Carson testifying against the misuse of pesticides before a Senate subcommittee

A committee of the National Academy of Sciences did not support Rachel's cause. However, a different conclusion was reached by the committee of the Office of Science and Technology — a special panel of the President's Science Advisory Committee. These scientists recognized the importance of *Silent Spring*. Industry and government agencies were criticized for not making public the dangers as well as the values of pesticides. However pleasing these words must have been to Rachel Carson, she wanted action. She testified before congressional committees, speaking as a biologist and emphasizing the need for environmental protection laws.

By 1963 *Silent Spring* had received public attention in Great Britain and had the endorsement of Prince Philip. In England, pesticides were not as widely used as in the United States, but their use had serious consequences. In a debate in the House of Lords, Lord Shackleton told of a cannibal who would not permit his tribe to eat Americans because their flesh was contaminated with chlorinated hydrocarbons. Since the English have only about 2 parts per million of DDT in their bodies while the Americans have 11 parts per million, Lord Shackleton joked that he was concerned about the export trade because now the English were more edible than the Americans. His humor brought more publicity to the problem than a serious presentation of the facts.

Silent Spring was soon published in fourteen other languages. Rachel Carson received many invitations to speak in other countries, but she was too sick to accept. She was in pain and weakened by radiation treatments. One honor that especially pleased her was the Schweitzer Medal of the Animal Welfare Institute. Albert Schweitzer's idea of reverence for life was one that she not only taught but also lived. All her life she rescued injured dogs, cared for stray cats, and returned her specimens to the sea after she had observed them.

Albert
Schweitzer

The National Council of Women
Of the United States
CITATION

Rachel Carson
Woman of Conscience

Because she is a distinguished scholar in the field of science ~~~

Because she is able to communicate her specialized knowledge ++++
through her impressive literary talent,

Because she has the courage to express her convictions in the +
face of powerful opposition,

Because she has shocked men and women into an awareness of their
responsibility to protect future generations, and finally,

Because with reverence for all life she dedicates her extraordinary
gifts to its service,

Therefore, the National Council of Women of the United States is proud
to cite RACHEL CARSON as the outstanding example in this
country of a Woman of Conscience

More honors came her way at the end of 1963. She received the Audubon Medal of the National Audubon Society, the Cullum Medal of the American Geographical Society, and perhaps most significant, was elected to membership in the American Academy of Arts and Sciences. The academy limited its membership to fifty, and in its entire history the academy had elected only about a dozen female members.

Rachel Carson died on April 14, 1964, when she was 56 years old. Just the September before, she had watched a flight of monarch butterflies with a friend. As a scientist, she realized that the butterflies—with a life span of only a few months—would not live to return from their migration. Yet Ms. Carson saw the ending of their lives at the end of their cycle of existence as a natural and not an unhappy thing. Rachel Carson wanted a passage from the end of *The Edge of the Sea* read at her funeral service. It concludes:

> And what is the meaning of so tiny a being as the transparent wisp of protoplasm that is a sea lace, existing for some reason inscrutable to us—a reason that demands its presence by the trillion amid the rocks and weeds of the shore? The meaning haunts and ever eludes us, and in its very pursuit we approach the ultimate mystery of Life itself.

Recognition of the significance of Rachel Carson's life has continued to grow. A National Wildlife Refuge in Maine was dedicated in her name. In 1981 a postage stamp bearing her picture was issued by the United States Postal Service. The nation's highest civilian honor, the Presidential Medal of Freedom, was awarded to her 16 years after her death. President Jimmy Carter presented the medal to Rachel Carson's adopted son, Roger Christie, with the following citation:

The President of the United States of America

Awards this

Presidential Medal of Freedom

to

Rachel Carson

Never silent herself in the face of destructive trends, Rachel Carson fed a spring of awareness across America and beyond. A biologist with a gentle, clear voice, she welcomed her audiences to her love of the sea, while with an equally clear determined voice she warned Americans of the dangers human beings themselves pose for their own environment. Always concerned, always eloquent, she created a tide of environmental consciousness that has not ebbed.

The White House
Washington, D.C., June 9, 1980

Jimmy Carter

Almost 30 years later, we can count many gains — thanks to the public support Rachel Carson's books helped to generate. But much work still remains if we are to protect the world in which we live.

Rachel shares her
lunch with a friend.

INDEX

About the Author:

Leila Merrell Foster is a lawyer, United Methodist minister, and clinical psychologist with degrees from Northwestern University and Garrett Evangelical Theological Seminary. She is the author of books and articles on a variety of subjects.